PERSPECTIVES ON
AMERICAN PROGRESS

ELEANOR ROOSEVELT

CHAMPIONS WOMEN'S RIGHTS

BY DUCHESS HARRIS, JD, PHD

with A. R. Carser

Core Library

Cover image: Eleanor Roosevelt promoted women's
rights her whole life.

An Imprint of Abdo Publishing
abdopublishing.com

abdopublishing.com

Published by Abdo Publishing, a division of ABDO, PO Box 398166, Minneapolis, Minnesota 55439. Copyright © 2019 by Abdo Consulting Group, Inc. International copyrights reserved in all countries. No part of this book may be reproduced in any form without written permission from the publisher. Core Library™ is a trademark and logo of Abdo Publishing.

Printed in the United States of America, North Mankato, Minnesota
022018
092018

THIS BOOK CONTAINS RECYCLED MATERIALS

Cover Photo: AP Images
Interior Photos: AP Images, 1, 9, 10–11, 13, 26, 36–37; Everett Collection, 4–5; Red Line Editorial, 16, 33; Bettmann/Getty Images, 18–19, 43; Everett Collection/Newscom, 22, 31; Green/AP Images, 28–29

Editor: Marie Pearson
Imprint Designer: Maggie Villaume
Series Design Direction: Ryan Gale

Library of Congress Control Number: 2017962649

Publisher's Cataloging-in-Publication Data

Names: Harris, Duchess, author. | Carser, A. R., author.
Title: Eleanor Roosevelt champions women's rights / by Duchess Harris and A. R. Carser.
Description: Minneapolis, Minnesota : Abdo Publishing, 2019. | Series: Perspectives on American progress | Includes online resources and index.
Identifiers: ISBN 9781532114892 (lib.bdg.) | ISBN 9781532154720 (ebook)
Subjects: LCSH: Roosevelt, Eleanor, 1884-1962--Juvenile literature. | Women's rights--Juvenile literature. | Women's rights--United States--History--20th century--Juvenile literature. | Presidents' spouses--United States--Juvenile literature.
Classification: DDC 973.917092 [B]--dc23

CONTENTS

CHAMPION OF EQUAL RIGHTS

A death threat from one of the nation's most notorious hate groups did not deter Eleanor Roosevelt. Roosevelt was the former First Lady and an advocate for women's, human, and civil rights. The Ku Klux Klan had discovered Roosevelt was planning to visit Highlander Folk School in Monteagle, Tennessee, in June 1958. She would speak on ways to protest racist laws. The Klan put a $25,000 bounty on her head.

But Roosevelt had spent her life helping marginalized women. Intimidation would not keep her away from Monteagle. Another woman picked Roosevelt up at the airport.

Roosevelt, *left*, promoted equal rights in society for both women and African Americans.

HIGHLANDER FOLK SCHOOL

Highlander Folk School was committed to causes including economic justice and an end to racial segregation. Courses included literacy, leadership, and nonviolent desegregation strategies. Notable activists including Rosa Parks attended classes there. Opponents of its causes tried to close the school.

They had a pistol in the car. They arrived in Monteagle without confronting the Klan.

In her national newspaper column "My Day," Roosevelt wrote of her time at Highlander Folk School. She had learned about the harsh rules states made for voters of color. This included African-American women. Women had gained the right to vote in 1920 with the Nineteenth Amendment. But state laws in the South made it nearly impossible for African Americans to vote. Roosevelt said people of different ethnicities could work together so all Americans could vote.

Equal Rights Advocate

Roosevelt was born in 1884. American women could not vote then. When Roosevelt was a teenager, women across the country fought for suffrage. The Nineteenth Amendment was just one step toward equal rights for women.

Roosevelt's family was wealthy and politically powerful. Eleanor's uncle Theodore Roosevelt was US president from 1901 to 1909. The Roosevelts helped Americans of all backgrounds.

This was especially true of Eleanor. From her late teens, she promoted equal rights for all Americans. She married rising political star Franklin Delano Roosevelt (FDR) in 1905. FDR was elected president in 1932, and Eleanor became the First Lady. This position gave Eleanor the ability to influence leaders. She secured more rights for women and minorities.

Her work did not stop after FDR's death in 1945. She advocated for women's right to work, affordable childcare, and housing in the 1950s and 1960s. And she stood with African Americans in the fight for civil rights. Roosevelt's work toward securing equal rights helped pave the way for future leaders.

Roosevelt's full name was Anna Eleanor Roosevelt.

DIFFERENT METHODS

Before 1920 women were not allowed to vote in most states. Suffragists had fought for the right since 1848. Roosevelt was one of those suffragists. In 1919, US Congress passed a Constitutional amendment to allow women to vote. Roosevelt had a reason to celebrate when three-quarters of US states approved the Nineteenth Amendment. All American women now had the right to vote.

With the right to vote secure, Roosevelt focused on new female voters. Roosevelt and other suffragists considered themselves

Roosevelt herself was an active voter. She and her family went to the polls together to vote for FDR as president.

New Women. New Women fought for better conditions for female workers. This included equal pay for men and women. They also fought for laws that protected women and children. Some organizations Roosevelt supported also advocated for a minimum wage. They supported health insurance for all Americans. Some encouraged women to participate in politics. This included voting. It also included running for public office.

Roosevelt's political connections helped her lobby lawmakers. She convinced them to write laws that supported these goals. She also spread the word in public. Her approach was careful. She did not choose to fight male lawmakers. She did not disrupt the way the government worked. Instead, she used her influence and power of persuasion. Her goal was to make gradual, lasting changes. This work may not have made headlines. But it did result in securing more rights for women.

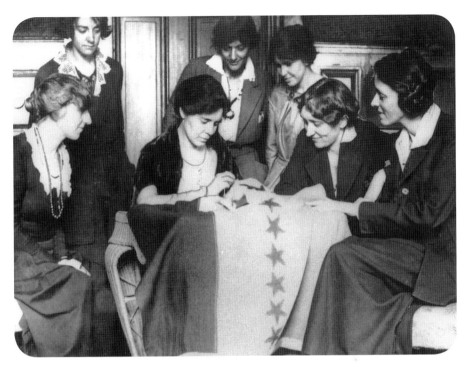

Alice Paul, *center*, sewed the 36th star on a banner. The stars represented the states that approved women's suffrage.

Making a Statement

Other women were more aggressive. Alice Paul was a leader of a more extreme group of activists. Like Roosevelt, Paul had fought most of her life for women's rights. But she and Roosevelt disagreed on the methods that would be most successful.

Paul believed women had to work outside the political system to create change. During the fight

WOODROW WILSON

Woodrow Wilson ran for president in 1912. Women's suffrage was only of passing interest to him. That changed when women from the National Woman's Party protested outside the White House. Onlooking men sometimes became violent toward the protesters. Law enforcement arrested the protesters. The activists refused to eat in jail. Their jailers force-fed them. This harsh treatment eventually persuaded Wilson. In 1918 he advocated for women's right to vote. At the time, the United States was fighting in World War I (1914–1918). Women were a vital part of the war workforce. If they could work for the war effort, Wilson argued, why refuse them the vote?

for the Nineteenth Amendment, Paul and other women staged protests outside the White House. Eventually, they were arrested. In jail they refused to eat. Their hunger strike made national news. It gained the sympathy of many Americans, including President Woodrow Wilson. The strike persuaded him to favor women's suffrage legislation. His support helped the Nineteenth Amendment pass.

Like Roosevelt, Paul shifted her focus after gaining the right to vote. But instead of gradual change, she advocated for a major shift in US political and social life. She wrote the Equal Rights Amendment (ERA) in 1923. If passed and ratified, it would enshrine equal rights for women in the US Constitution. Paul's amendment made it to Congress. But it was not passed. In 1972, the ERA finally passed both houses of Congress. It went to the states for approval. But it never gained enough support.

WHO WAS ALICE PAUL?

Alice Paul grew up in a politically active family. She traveled to England in 1907. While there, she experienced her first protest and hunger strike. They were successful in Europe. When she returned to the United States, Paul brought the more extreme methods with her. She and other women founded the National Woman's Party in 1916. This group staged protests in front of the White House. Paul spent the rest of her life fighting for the passage of the ERA. She died in 1977.

APPROVING THE
ERA

As of March 22, 2017, 36 of the needed 38 states had approved the ERA. Six other states were considering ERA bills. The map above shows the states that have not approved it. Why do you think it took until 2017 for some states to approve the ERA?

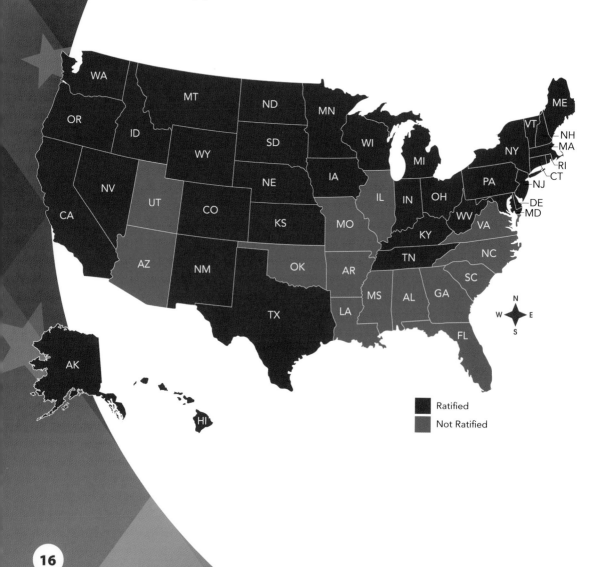

Ratified

Not Ratified

Paul refused to join an established political party. She argued the male-dominated Democratic and Republican parties would eventually betray women. Roosevelt, however, was an active member of the Democratic Party. She experienced first-hand the party's reluctant embrace of women's issues. Instead of withdrawing and starting her own party, Roosevelt fought to change it. She worked for the party. She became head of the women's division in 1923. She pressured influential Democrats to include more women when picking candidates. This approach would define Roosevelt's work for the rest of her life.

EXPLORE ONLINE

Chapter Two discusses Alice Paul's approach to changing the nation. The website below tells more about her life and work. What information does the website give about how Paul worked to bring about changes? Does the article answer any questions you had about Paul's methods?

CHILDREN'S BIOGRAPHY OF ALICE PAUL

abdocorelibrary.com/eleanor-roosevelt

THE WHITE HOUSE

In 1932, FDR won the US presidential election. Roosevelt struggled to find her stride in the White House. Then friend and journalist Lorena Hickok stepped in. Hickok was frustrated. Female journalists did not have easy access to the president. They were banned from the president's press conferences. Hickok asked Roosevelt for help.

Roosevelt came up with an idea. She would hold press conferences as First Lady. Only female journalists would be allowed. Female reporters looked at and wrote about the news from a female perspective. They asked questions men would not think to ask.

Female journalists gathered to listen to Roosevelt's exclusive press conferences.

Their stories would be exclusives. They would also appeal to female readers and voters.

Roosevelt's solution worked. She first took the podium on March 6, 1933. The room was packed. Women sat on the floor in front of the podium to hear her speak. Roosevelt said that a female reporter's job was to tell readers what they thought was important. They influenced important women in the United States.

At first male reporters scoffed at being excluded. So did FDR's press secretary. But soon they were begging female reporters for the latest story. Roosevelt's press conferences improved women's access to the White House. But they did not include all female journalists. The White House still banned African American reporters. It said this was because African American reporters worked for weekly instead of daily papers.

Women in the Workforce

Women across the country were suffering when FDR was elected. The Great Depression had started in 1929. Millions of Americans were out of work. Those who had jobs saw pay cuts. Many male workers had lost jobs. But the country needed telephone operators, nurses, and teachers. Women mostly held these jobs. In many homes, women now made money for the family.

But federal law had not caught up to this reality. Families could not have more than one adult working for

Camp Tera in New York was one of the camps Roosevelt, *center*, had set up for women.

the federal government. Some programs banned female workers. Others hired women only for traditionally female jobs such as cleaning. Women were paid less than men for the same type of work. African-American women were often refused employment entirely.

Roosevelt found these injustices frustrating. She was often at odds with FDR and his administration. In 1933, FDR created a work program called the Civilian Conservation Corps (CCC). The men developing the program banned women from it. Roosevelt protested, saying women should be included. She campaigned for a program for women only. FDR's administration did not like this idea. But Roosevelt persevered. By 1936, she had started 90 women-only work camps. They served 5,000 women a year by 1936.

The New Deal

Roosevelt succeeded in other ways. Her husband's administration passed a group of programs called the New Deal. It created new rules for banks. It provided help for unemployed Americans.

Roosevelt helped boost public support for the New Deal. An illness had left FDR unable to walk. This made travel across the country very difficult. Roosevelt stepped in. She spoke to women of all ethnicities about

SUPPORTING A STAR

Marian Anderson was a world-famous opera star. Howard University invited Anderson to sing at Constitution Hall in Washington, DC. But Anderson was an African-American woman. Constitution Hall, owned by the Daughters of the American Revolution (DAR), banned African Americans. Roosevelt was a member of DAR. She was outraged by the ban. She resigned from DAR immediately. But DAR did not change its mind. So Roosevelt found Anderson a new venue. On April 9, 1939, Anderson took the stage in front of the Lincoln Memorial. Up to 75,000 people were there to hear Anderson sing. She opened the outdoor concert with "My Country, 'Tis of Thee."

the programs. The pace was grueling. She stopped at schools and factories across the United States. Once New Deal programs were in place, she traveled again. She checked how the programs were working.

Roosevelt learned a lot during her travels. She saw the working conditions of women and African Americans. She pressured FDR to include women, African Americans, and young adults in New Deal programs. He did. By the end of his presidency, FDR had included more women and African Americans in federal programs and jobs than any other US president.

War Begins

During FDR's first term, the economy began to improve. The New Deal programs had provided jobs and support to American families. The success earned FDR three more terms in 1936, 1940, and 1944. During this time, World War II (1939–1945) had begun in Europe. Some countries looked to the United States for help. The United States provided the United Kingdom with much-needed military supplies. This boosted the US manufacturing industry.

Then tragedy struck. On December 7, 1941, Japanese bombers attacked a US naval base in Pearl Harbor, Hawaii. The United States entered World War II the next day. Millions of American men traveled across the oceans to fight. At home, women filled jobs men left behind. They helped make planes, battleships, and

Roosevelt met with American women who worked as pilots during the war. They flew aircraft to fighter pilots who needed them.

ammunition. At home, they collected scrap rubber and metal to supply the war effort.

Roosevelt supported women in the war workforce. She advocated for labor and civil rights reforms for wartime workers. She visited troops overseas.

Her advocacy rubbed some in FDR's office the wrong way. One aide asked her why she did so many controversial things. "I have access to the president," she responded. "And if [I didn't] use that access to do things that need to be done . . . for people, I would be sorely remiss and irresponsible."

FURTHER EVIDENCE

Chapter Three discusses Roosevelt's influence on FDR's presidency. What was one of the main points of this chapter? What evidence is included to support this point? Read the article at the website below. Does the information on the website support the main point of the chapter? Does it present new evidence?

ELEANOR ROOSEVELT: NO ORDINARY WOMAN
abdocorelibrary.com/eleanor-roosevelt

ENLARGING THE TENT

FDR died on April 12, 1945. He was still in office. His vice president Harry Truman was sworn in the same day. But Roosevelt's women's rights work continued. And she drew even more people under the equal rights tent.

Rights for All

By 1947 Roosevelt had spent more than four decades fighting for women's equal rights. That year she expanded her fight. She worked to declare the rights of all people. The United Nations (UN) had formed in 1945. It is an organization of nations that aims to keep peace and protect human rights. It created the

Roosevelt was a US delegate to the United Nations from 1945 to 1952.

Commission on Human Rights. The commission would draft a Universal Declaration of Human Rights. It would explain basic human rights.

There were 18 countries on the commission. President Truman knew who to send to represent the United States. Roosevelt was a perfect fit. She was the only woman in the group. She made sure women were included in the declaration. Roosevelt was also the chair of the group. She helped the group work together to write a definition for human rights. In September 1948, the commission gave its draft to the UN. The UN debated changes. In December, the assembly met in Paris, France, to vote. Eight nations did not vote. But no nation voted against the declaration. It was approved. Roosevelt received a standing ovation for her hard work.

The Fight Continues at Home

During her UN work, Roosevelt wrote her popular "My Day" newspaper column. She became more vocal

Roosevelt, *center*, led the Commission on Human Rights. Other countries involved included China, the Soviet Union, France, and India.

about civil rights for African Americans. Roosevelt wrote against racism in laws and government. In a country dominated by white men, African-American women were discriminated against for both their race and their gender.

Roosevelt spent the 1950s working for civil rights and human rights. But in 1961, she refocused on women. President John F. Kennedy asked her to chair his Commission on the Status of Women in December. Under her leadership, the commission investigated how women were treated in education, in the workplace, and in US law. The group looked at laws that decided pay and hours. The final report, called the Peterson Report, showed discrimination

PERSPECTIVES

PAULI MURRAY AND ELEANOR ROOSEVELT

Pauli Murray was an African-American attorney enrolled in a New Deal program. She was outraged when FDR spoke at an all-white college. She sent a letter to him expressing her anger. She also sent a copy to Eleanor Roosevelt. It sparked a decades-long friendship. Roosevelt was more willing than her husband to advocate for civil rights. Murray wrote Roosevelt a letter shortly before Roosevelt's death. Part of it read: "Two generations of women have been touched by your spirit."

PETERSON REPORT PROGRESS

	What It Means	Where It Stands in 2017
Education for Adult Women	Make education and training for working-age women accessible and affordable	Women make up more than half of all undergraduate students
Equal Opportunity Employment	Private employers should provide women an equal chance to be hired, trained, and promoted	Equal opportunity employment laws forbid employers from discriminating against women, minorities, and other protected groups
Equal Pay for Equal Work	States should require women be paid the same as men for the same jobs	Equal Pay Act requires men and women at the same workplace to be paid the same amount of money for the same work
Paid Maternity Leave	Pay new mothers while they are on leave after giving birth	No federally required paid maternity leave

It has been more than 50 years since the Commission on the Status of Women published the Peterson Report. Here is where the United States stands on its key recommendations. Why do you think some of these have been addressed more than others?

against working women. It offered ways to improve the problem. These included paid maternity leave for new mothers and childcare for all working women.

UNSUNG HEROES OF THE CIVIL RIGHTS MOVEMENT

For decades, women's contributions to the civil rights movement went unrecognized. But thousands of women fought for civil rights for African Americans. They were lawyers, local organizers, and individual protesters. Mildred Bond Roxborough was a secretary for the National Association for the Advancement of Colored People (NAACP). She recalls that without women, there would be no NAACP. Women organized local branches and set up meetings. Ruby Nell Sales stresses the movement needed working women, too. Maids and other female service workers boycotted buses and attended protests.

Roosevelt enjoyed the work. But she found it more difficult to keep up her grueling pace. In 1962 Roosevelt became ill. She died on November 7, 1962. The commission published the final report in October 1963. Among its first pages was a tribute to Roosevelt.

STRAIGHT TO THE
SOURCE

The Universal Declaration of Human Rights made the following statements about equality in Articles 1–3:

Article 1

All human beings are born free and equal in dignity and rights. They are endowed with reason and conscience and should act towards one another in a spirit of brotherhood.

Article 2

Everyone is entitled to all the rights and freedoms set forth in this Declaration, without distinction of any kind, such as race, colour, sex, language, religion, political or other opinion, national or social origin, property, birth or other status. . . .

Article 3

Everyone has the right to life, liberty and security of person.

Source: "Women's Rights: Eleanor Roosevelt." *National Park Service.* US Department of the Interior, February 26, 2015. Web. Accessed November 6, 2017.

What's the Big Idea?
Take a close look at this passage. What is the main point of the three articles? Why do you think the commission decided to include these rights as the first three articles of the Declaration?

ROOSEVELT'S LEGACY

Roosevelt passed away one year before Betty Friedan published *The Feminine Mystique*. This book sparked a new wave of feminism in the 1960s and 1970s. Women across the country took up the fight for equal rights. They wanted an end to discrimination in the workplace. They marched to protest sexism in American society. They renewed the fight for the ERA.

Roosevelt did not live to see this new movement. But she had worked all her life to make it possible. She wanted women to speak their minds and vote for what they believed. That is exactly what American women of all

Friedan encouraged women to become independent of their husbands by working and doing other things outside of traditional female roles.

ethnicities started to do. A new kind of women's rights activist emerged. These women reflected on the activists who came before them. Some believed Roosevelt did not earn the right to be called a feminist. Others disagreed.

Not a Feminist

Some feminist scholars today are critical of Roosevelt's work. They acknowledge her contribution to improving women's working conditions and passing protective laws for women. But they argue Roosevelt did not search for the reasons why sexism existed. Instead, she focused on making steps toward protecting women's basic rights.

Roosevelt also opposed the ERA. She believed it would take away the protective laws she had fought years for. After two decades of fighting it, Roosevelt came to support the amendment in the 1950s. Some believe Roosevelt could not have been a feminist because of her opposition to the ERA.

A Feminist

However, other feminist scholars disagree. The challenges facing women in the 1920s and 1930s were different from those in the 1960s. These scholars argue that Roosevelt spent four decades fighting for laws to protect women's rights and equality. Gloria Steinem was an influential leader of the women's

SECOND-WAVE FEMINISM

The women's movement of the 1960s and 1970s is considered part of the second wave of American feminism. The first wave occurred in the late 1800s and early 1900s. One thing second-wave feminism focused on was passing the ERA. The movement was more inclusive of women of color and low-income women. These groups had been left out of first-wave feminism.

movement. She noted that Roosevelt worked hard to help women in politics and at home.

Roosevelt's supporters acknowledge she did not support the ERA for much of her life. But her views changed. She eventually supported the amendment. Friedan said in 1984 that contemporary feminists should not judge Roosevelt on her opposition to the ERA. Friedan explained that Roosevelt feared the ERA would undo all of her past work.

Today feminists have the same disagreements Paul and Roosevelt did in the 1920s and 1930s. Some feminists want to take aggressive action to improve women's rights. Others want to work within the existing government system. As Paul and Roosevelt demonstrated, both approaches can be effective. For most feminists today, Roosevelt's accomplishments speak for themselves. Her contributions to women's, civil, and human rights continue to help empower women and girls today.

STRAIGHT TO THE
SOURCE

Roosevelt wrote an article for *Home* magazine in March 1932. In it, she encourages women to act on their political values and desires. She ends her article with these two thoughts:

> *If ten million women really want security, real representation, honesty, wise and just legislation, happier and more comfortable conditions of living, and a future with the horrors of war removed from the horizon, then these ten million women must bestir themselves.*

> *They can be active factors in the life of their communities and shape the future, or they can drift along and hide behind the men. Today is a challenge to women. Tomorrow will see how they answer the challenge!*

> Source: Eleanor Roosevelt. "What Ten Million Women Want." *The Eleanor Roosevelt Papers Project*. George Washington University, n.d. Web. Accessed November 6, 2017.

Consider Your Audience

Adapt this passage for a different audience, such as your principal or friends. Write a blog post conveying this same information for the new audience. How does your post differ from the original text and why?

IMPORTANT
DATES

1884
Roosevelt is born in New York.

1920
The Nineteenth Amendment is approved by the states and becomes law on August 26.

1923
Alice Paul's Equal Rights Amendment is introduced in Congress for the first time.

1929
The Great Depression begins in the United States.

1932
Franklin Delano Roosevelt wins the presidential election.

1945
FDR dies on April 12 while he is still in office.

1948
The UN General Assembly adopts the Universal Declaration of Human Rights.

1958
Roosevelt travels to Monteagle, Tennessee, in June despite a $25,000 bounty on her head from the Ku Klux Klan.

1962
Roosevelt dies on November 7.

STOP AND
THINK

Surprise Me

Chapter Two discusses the fight for women's rights in the 1920s. After reading this book, what two or three facts about the early women's rights movement surprised you? Write a few sentences about each fact. Why did you find each fact surprising?

Dig Deeper

After reading this book, what questions do you still have about Eleanor Roosevelt's work in women's rights? With an adult's help, find a few reliable sources that can help you answer your questions. Write a paragraph about what you learned.

Take a Stand

Chapter Five presents Roosevelt's work from two different viewpoints. Reread this chapter, then take a side. Do you think Roosevelt was a feminist? Or do you think she did not do enough to earn that title? Why?

GLOSSARY

bounty
money given to someone who captures a wanted person

civil rights
a citizen's rights outside of the political realm

commission
a group of people asked to perform a specific task

discrimination
action that treats people differently based on traits such as race or gender

feminism
the idea that women are equal to men politically, economically, and socially

legislation
laws made by a political body such as Congress

lobby
represent and argue for a particular group to influence politicians

marginalized
made unable to influence society or considered unimportant

press conference
an announcement and interview someone gives to the press

reform
a change or improvement

suffrage
the right to vote

wage
a regular payment given for work performed

ONLINE
RESOURCES

To learn more about Eleanor Roosevelt, visit our free resource websites below.

Visit **abdocorelibrary.com** for free Common Core resources for teachers and students, including vetted activities, multimedia, and booklinks, for deeper subject comprehension.

Visit **abdobooklinks.com** for free additional online weblinks for further learning. These links are routinely monitored and updated to provide the most current information available.

LEARN
MORE

Caldwell, Stella, et al. *100 Women Who Made History: Remarkable Women Who Shaped Our World*. New York: DK, 2017.

Conley, Kate. *World War II through the Eyes of Franklin Delano Roosevelt*. Minneapolis, MN: Abdo, 2016.

Harris, Duchess. *Women's Suffrage*. Minneapolis, MN: Abdo, 2018.

ABOUT THE
AUTHORS

Duchess Harris, JD, PhD
Professor Harris is the chair of the American Studies department at Macalester College and curator of the Duchess Harris Collection of ABDO books. She is the author and coauthor of recently released ABDO books including *Hidden Human Computers: The Black Women of NASA*, *Black Lives Matter*, and *Race and Policing*.

Before working with ABDO, she authored several other books on the topics of race, culture, and American history. She served as an associate editor for *Litigation News*, the American Bar Association Section of Litigation's quarterly flagship publication, and was the first editor in chief of *Law Raza*, an interactive online journal covering race and the law, published at William Mitchell College of Law. She has earned a PhD in American Studies from the University of Minnesota and a JD from William Mitchell College of Law.

A. R. Carser
A. R. Carser is a freelance writer who lives in Minnesota. She enjoys learning and writing about US history, culture, and society.

INDEX